M000218571

If found, please contact...

Name: _____

Email: _____

Phone Number: _____

Important Info...

Passport Number: _____

Issue Date: _____ Expiry Date: _____

KTN (Known Traveler Number)* _____

*A KTN is issued if you sign up for Global Entry, NEXUS, and SENTRI, programs of U.S. Customs and Border Protection. Use your membership number as a "known traveler number" in airline reservations to receive TSA PreCheck.

International Travel Journal
Copyright 2021© Michael Wedaa
All rights reserved.

ISBN: 978-1-7360629-1-3

Congratulations on your purchase of the *International Travel Journal*. I hope you get a lot of value out of recording your unique travel memories so that you can revisit them often over time.

To thank you for purchasing this journal, I am giving away some FREE travel tools that will help make your next travel adventure even better.

Go to www.internationaltravelsecrets.com/travel-tools

There you will find FREE resources such as these:

- Best travel credit cards
- Layover planning checklist
- Best and worst airlines
- Travel packing list
- Links to helpful visa and entry requirement sites
- Quiz: which region of the world fits your personality?

And much more!

Be sure to check out my ONLINE TRAVEL COURSE!

Happy traveling!

A PERFECT COMPANION TO THE BEST-SELLING BOOK
International Travel Secrets

International Travel Secrets has step-by-step instructions on finding rock-bottom prices on travel--without booking last minute or staying in crowded hostels. A must-read for beginning travelers and seasoned travelers alike. Find out how to see a country in 2 days and how to use layovers as a tool to see more countries--for free! Learn how to avoid baggage fees, ATM fees, and foreign transaction fees. Master how to determine which countries are safe and how to protect yourself in a robbery. Learn how to negotiate prices, which credit cards to use, how to get free travel insurance, and much more!

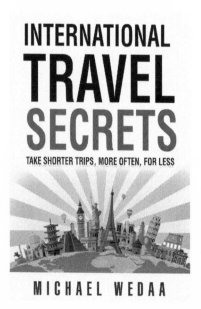

INTERNATIONAL
TRAVEL
SECRETS
TAKE SHORTER TRIPS, MORE OFTEN, FOR LESS

MICHAEL WEDAA

Packing List

Most Important Items

- [ ] Passport
- [ ] Photocopy of passport in your luggage
- [ ] Email a copy of your passport to yourself
- [ ] Visas for the countries you are visiting
- [ ] Universal outlet adapter (electrical outlets are different on each continent)
- [ ] Phone charger
- [ ] External phone charger (that can fully charge your phone 2-3 times)
- [ ] Pen (for filling out arrival cards at customs)

Personal Items

- [ ] Shampoo, deodorant, soap
- [ ] Toothbrush & toothpaste
- [ ] Toilet paper
- [ ] Sunscreen
- [ ] Trash bag (to separate dirty clothes in your luggage)
- [ ] Dryer sheets (to keep clothes smelling fresh)
- [ ] Zip-lock bags for shampoo, sunscreen, etc. (yes sometimes they leak!)
- [ ] Headphones for airplane (so you don't have to purchase them on the flight)
- [ ] Books (to pass time on flights)

Packing List

Business Items

- ❏ **ATM cards**
  (for fee-free cards, see the Foreign Currency chapter in *International Travel Secrets* book)
- ❏ **Credit cards**
  (for foreign transaction fee-free cards, see Credit Cards chapter in *International Travel Secrets* book)
- ❏ **Throw-away wallet**
  (see Safety chapter in *International Travel Secrets* book)
- ❏ **Laptop, Laptop charger**

Clothes

- ❏ **Running shoes** (mine are black and double as semi-dress shoes)
- ❏ **Flip-flops**
- ❏ **Jeans**
- ❏ **Shorts**
- ❏ **Socks**
- ❏ **Underwear**
- ❏ **Bathing suit**
- ❏ **Jacket or sweatshirt** (depending upon weather conditions)
- ❏ **Belt**
- ❏ **Sunglasses**
- ❏ **Hat**

Trip Planner

- ❏ Airline/Flight Number/Time
- ❏ Price
- ❏ Layover Hours

- ❏ Visa needed for entry?
- ❏ Vaccinations needed for entry?
- ❏ Local Currency Name and Conversion

- ❏ Uber/Taxi/Train from airport to hotel
- ❏ Average cost of ground transportation
- ❏ Time to city center

- ❏ Hotel Name
- ❏ Check in/check out time
- ❏ Refundable?

- ❏ Attractions and landmarks I want to see
- ❏ Tour information

- ❏ Local Scams
- ❏ Country Safety Rating

(https://travel.state.gov/content/travel/en/international-travel/International-Travel-Country-Information-Pages.html)

What was the best part of today?

This question is meant to keep your focus on the positive experiences. Even if you had a bad day, this question will help shift your thoughts to something that occurred that you enjoyed.

What was the best meal I had?

This question will help you remember some new food you tried from a street vendor or maybe even remember a good restaurant to visit once you return to the location at some later date.

What was better than I expected?

Like the first question, this also helps you to focus on positive experiences, but in a different manner. Every journey has some experience that surpasses our expectations. For me, it was seeing the Taj Mahal for the first time with my own eyes. Pictures of this beautiful wonder simply do not do it justice.

Whom did I meet today?

You may have had a great interaction with a private tour guide, with another traveler, or even a local. Log that interaction here.

What did my travel partner enjoy the most? Why?

This question allows you to engage with your travel partner (if you are not braving the road alone) to get a different perspective on an experience that you may not have thought of yourself.

What do I want to see more of?

This helps you remember something that you may want to revisit. It is customary for us to feel rushed on guided tours and sometimes you may want to return to a particular place to spend more time exploring. Document those locations here.

Additional Thoughts

Use this space to jot down any other thoughts you may want to record or to document something that is not covered in any of the other prompts.

What am I missing most from home?

We all miss simple pleasures of home while on the road. Use this section to document whether you miss your pet, a type of food, your back patio, your bed, clean bathrooms, etc.

What am I going to eat first when I return home?

I always enjoy creating a list of guilty pleasures I want to enjoy, sometimes right after leaving the airport once I return to my home city. Make a list of those foods you've been missing the most.

What new things will I try when I return home?

Use this section to create a list of new things you will try once you return home. While traveling, I often come up with ideas of places to visit once I return home--a park, a local museum I often see, or a bike trail. . . all places I pass while driving near home, but have never taken the time to visit.

Whom will I visit when I return home?

List friends, co-workers, or family members you haven't visited in a while, maybe because both of you are "too busy" to make plans.

What personal / self-improvement tasks will I complete?

Traveling allows you the freedom to move past the clutter in your mind and think more freely and creatively, inspiring you to take action when you return home.

The following pages give examples of how to populate this journal.

What was the best part of today?

We met a restaurant owner who disapproved of what we ordered, so he called the waiter over and had him bring us dishes he wanted us to try--for free!

What was the best meal I had?

Cabernet Franc and Turkish sausage

What was better than I expected?

1. *The ferry ride over the Bosphorus Strait*
2. *View from Galata Tower*
3. *The Turkish Wine*

Whom did I meet today?

We met a nice couple traveling from Algeria

What did my travel partner enjoy the most? Why?

He liked the Medusa heads in the underground Roman cistern--they were built 1500 years ago!

What do I want to see more of?

I would like to explore more of the food places in the neighborhood near Galata Tower

Additional Thoughts

I loved the mixed history of the city--remnants of the Roman Empire and the Ottoman Turks can be seen in both the architecture and food. This city truly is a gateway between Central Asia & Eastern Europe

What am I missing most from home?

1. *In-N-Out burgers*
2. *My own bed*
3. *Visiting my family*

What am I going to eat first when I return home?

Lobster tacos at Rubio's

What new things will I try when I return home?

Visit a local museum, hike a new trail

Whom will I visit when I return home?

An old co-worker, my fifth grade teacher

What personal / self-improvement tasks will I complete?

Read 2 new books, do yoga 3x per week, play guitar everyday, meditate 3x per week, walk everyday

What was the best part of today?

_____

_____

What was the best meal I had?

_____

What was better than I expected?

    1.

    2.

    3.

Whom did I meet today?

_____

What did my travel partner enjoy the most? Why?

_____

_____

What do I want to see more of?

_____

_____

What was the best part of today?

_____

_____

What was the best meal I had?

_____

What was better than I expected?

   1.

   2.

   3.

Whom did I meet today?

_____

What did my travel partner enjoy the most? Why?

_____

_____

What do I want to see more of?

_____

_____

Date: Location:

What was the best part of today?

_____

_____

What was the best meal I had?

_____

What was better than I expected?

   1.

   2.

   3.

Whom did I meet today?

_____

What did my travel partner enjoy the most? Why?

_____

_____

What do I want to see more of?

_____

_____

Additional Thoughts

_____

_____

_____

_____

What am I missing most from home?

   1.

   2.

   3.

What am I going to eat first when I return home?

_____

What new things will I try when I return home?

_____

Whom will I visit when I return home?

_____

What personal / self-improvement tasks will I complete?

_____

_____

"I cannot think of anything that excites a greater sense of childlike wonder than to be in a country where you are ignorant of almost anything. Suddenly you are five years old again. You can't read anything, you have only the most rudimentary sense of how things work, you can't reliably cross a street without endangering your life. Your whole existence becomes a series of interesting guesses."

– Bill Bryson

Date: **Location:**

What was the best part of today?

_____

_____

What was the best meal I had?

_____

What was better than I expected?

1.

2.

3.

Whom did I meet today?

_____

What did my travel partner enjoy the most? Why?

_____

_____

What do I want to see more of?

_____

_____

What was the best part of today?

_____

_____

What was the best meal I had?

_____

What was better than I expected?

   1.

   2.

   3.

Whom did I meet today?

_____

What did my travel partner enjoy the most? Why?

_____

_____

What do I want to see more of?

_____

_____

What was the best part of today?

_____

_____

What was the best meal I had?

_____

What was better than I expected?

    1.

    2.

    3.

Whom did I meet today?

_____

What did my travel partner enjoy the most? Why?

_____

_____

What do I want to see more of?

_____

_____

Additional Thoughts

_____

_____

_____

_____

What am I missing most from home?

1.

2.

3.

What am I going to eat first when I return home?

_____

What new things will I try when I return home?

_____

Whom will I visit when I return home?

_____

What personal / self-improvement tasks will I complete?

_____

_____

"Travel isn't always pretty. It isn't always comfortable. Sometimes it hurts, it even breaks your heart. But that's okay. The journey changes you; it should change you. It leaves marks on your memory, on your consciousness, on your heart, and on your body. You take something with you. Hopefully, you leave something good behind."

– Anthony Bourdain

What was the best part of today?

_____

_____

What was the best meal I had?

_____

What was better than I expected?

    1.

    2.

    3.

Whom did I meet today?

_____

What did my travel partner enjoy the most? Why?

_____

_____

What do I want to see more of?

_____

_____

What was the best part of today?

_____

_____

What was the best meal I had?

_____

What was better than I expected?

1.

2.

3.

Whom did I meet today?

_____

What did my travel partner enjoy the most? Why?

_____

_____

What do I want to see more of?

_____

_____

What was the best part of today?

_____

_____

What was the best meal I had?

_____

What was better than I expected?

    1.

    2.

    3.

Whom did I meet today?

_____

What did my travel partner enjoy the most? Why?

_____

_____

What do I want to see more of?

_____

_____

Additional Thoughts

_____

_____

_____

_____

What am I missing most from home?

    1.

    2.

    3.

What am I going to eat first when I return home?

_____

What new things will I try when I return home?

_____

Whom will I visit when I return home?

_____

What personal / self-improvement tasks will I complete?

_____

_____

"What you've done becomes the judge of what you're going to do—especially in other people's minds. When you're traveling, you are what you are right there and then. People don't have your past to hold against you. No Yesterdays on the road."

– William Least Heat-Moon

What was the best part of today?

_____

_____

What was the best meal I had?

_____

What was better than I expected?

    1.

    2.

    3.

Whom did I meet today?

_____

What did my travel partner enjoy the most? Why?

_____

_____

What do I want to see more of?

_____

_____

Date: Location:

What was the best part of today?

_____

_____

What was the best meal I had?

_____

What was better than I expected?

1.

2.

3.

Whom did I meet today?

_____

What did my travel partner enjoy the most? Why?

_____

_____

What do I want to see more of?

_____

_____

What was the best part of today?

_____

_____

What was the best meal I had?

_____

What was better than I expected?

   1.

   2.

   3.

Whom did I meet today?

_____

What did my travel partner enjoy the most? Why?

_____

_____

What do I want to see more of?

_____

_____

Additional Thoughts

_____

_____

_____

_____

What am I missing most from home?

1.

2.

3.

What am I going to eat first when I return home?

_____

What new things will I try when I return home?

_____

Whom will I visit when I return home?

_____

What personal / self-improvement tasks will I complete?

_____

_____

"Twenty years from now you will be more disappointed by the things you didn't do than by the ones you did do. So throw off the bowlines, sail away from the safe harbor. Catch the trade winds in your sails. Explore. Dream. Discover."

– **Mark Twain**

What was the best part of today?

_____

_____

What was the best meal I had?

_____

What was better than I expected?

1.

2.

3.

Whom did I meet today?

_____

What did my travel partner enjoy the most? Why?

_____

_____

What do I want to see more of?

_____

_____

What was the best part of today?

_____

_____

What was the best meal I had?

_____

What was better than I expected?

    1.

    2.

    3.

Whom did I meet today?

_____

What did my travel partner enjoy the most? Why?

_____

_____

What do I want to see more of?

_____

_____

What was the best part of today?

_____

_____

What was the best meal I had?

_____

What was better than I expected?

    1.

    2.

    3.

Whom did I meet today?

_____

What did my travel partner enjoy the most? Why?

_____

_____

What do I want to see more of?

_____

_____

Additional Thoughts

_____

_____

_____

_____

What am I missing most from home?

1.

2.

3.

What am I going to eat first when I return home?

_____

What new things will I try when I return home?

_____

Whom will I visit when I return home?

_____

What personal / self-improvement tasks will I complete?

_____

_____

"Travelling is a brutality. It forces you to trust strangers and to lose sight of all that familiar comfort of home and friends. You are constantly off balance. Nothing is yours except the essential things--air, sleep, dreams, the sea, the sky--all things tending towards the eternal or what we imagine of it."

– Cesare Pavese

What was the best part of today?

_____

_____

What was the best meal I had?

_____

What was better than I expected?

1.

2.

3.

Whom did I meet today?

_____

What did my travel partner enjoy the most? Why?

_____

_____

What do I want to see more of?

_____

_____

What was the best part of today?

_____

_____

What was the best meal I had?

_____

What was better than I expected?

1.

2.

3.

Whom did I meet today?

_____

What did my travel partner enjoy the most? Why?

_____

_____

What do I want to see more of?

_____

_____

What was the best part of today?

_____

_____

What was the best meal I had?

_____

What was better than I expected?

    1.

    2.

    3.

Whom did I meet today?

_____

What did my travel partner enjoy the most? Why?

_____

_____

What do I want to see more of?

_____

_____

Additional Thoughts

_____

_____

_____

_____

What am I missing most from home?

1.

2.

3.

What am I going to eat first when I return home?

_____

What new things will I try when I return home?

_____

Whom will I visit when I return home?

_____

What personal / self-improvement tasks will I complete?

_____

_____

"I rather believe that time is a companion who goes with us on the journey and reminds us to cherish every moment because they'll never come again. What we leave behind is not as important as how we have lived."

– Jean-Luc Picard

Date: **Location:**

What was the best part of today?

_____

_____

What was the best meal I had?

_____

What was better than I expected?

    1.

    2.

    3.

Whom did I meet today?

_____

What did my travel partner enjoy the most? Why?

_____

_____

What do I want to see more of?

_____

_____

What was the best part of today?

_____

_____

What was the best meal I had?

_____

What was better than I expected?

1.

2.

3.

Whom did I meet today?

_____

What did my travel partner enjoy the most? Why?

_____

_____

What do I want to see more of?

_____

_____

What was the best part of today?

_____

_____

What was the best meal I had?

_____

What was better than I expected?

1.

2.

3.

Whom did I meet today?

_____

What did my travel partner enjoy the most? Why?

_____

_____

What do I want to see more of?

_____

_____

*"Collect moments, not things." – **Anonymous***

Additional Thoughts

_____

_____

_____

_____

What am I missing most from home?

1.

2.

3.

What am I going to eat first when I return home?

_____

What new things will I try when I return home?

_____

Whom will I visit when I return home?

_____

What personal / self-improvement tasks will I complete?

_____

_____

"What you have to decide... is how you want your life to be. If your forever was ending tomorrow, would this be how you'd want to have spent it? Listen, the truth is, nothing is guaranteed. So don't be afraid, be alive."

– Sarah Dessen

What was the best part of today?

_____

_____

What was the best meal I had?

_____

What was better than I expected?

1.

2.

3.

Whom did I meet today?

_____

What did my travel partner enjoy the most? Why?

_____

_____

What do I want to see more of?

_____

_____

What was the best part of today?

_____

_____

What was the best meal I had?

_____

What was better than I expected?

   1.

   2.

   3.

Whom did I meet today?

_____

What did my travel partner enjoy the most? Why?

_____

_____

What do I want to see more of?

_____

_____

What was the best part of today?

_____

_____

What was the best meal I had?

_____

What was better than I expected?

    1.

    2.

    3.

Whom did I meet today?

_____

What did my travel partner enjoy the most? Why?

_____

_____

What do I want to see more of?

_____

_____

Additional Thoughts

_____

_____

_____

_____

What am I missing most from home?

1.

2.

3.

What am I going to eat first when I return home?

_____

What new things will I try when I return home?

_____

Whom will I visit when I return home?

_____

What personal / self-improvement tasks will I complete?

_____

_____

"To move, to breathe, to fly, to float,
To gain all while you give,
To roam the roads of lands remote,
To travel is to live."

– Hans Christian Andersen

What was the best part of today?

_____

_____

What was the best meal I had?

_____

What was better than I expected?

    1.

    2.

    3.

Whom did I meet today?

_____

What did my travel partner enjoy the most? Why?

_____

_____

What do I want to see more of?

_____

_____

What was the best part of today?

_____

_____

What was the best meal I had?

_____

What was better than I expected?

1.

2.

3.

Whom did I meet today?

_____

What did my travel partner enjoy the most? Why?

_____

_____

What do I want to see more of?

_____

_____

Date: **Location:**

What was the best part of today?

_____

_____

What was the best meal I had?

_____

What was better than I expected?

1.

2.

3.

Whom did I meet today?

_____

What did my travel partner enjoy the most? Why?

_____

_____

What do I want to see more of?

_____

_____

Additional Thoughts

_____

_____

_____

_____

What am I missing most from home?

1.

2.

3.

What am I going to eat first when I return home?

_____

What new things will I try when I return home?

_____

Whom will I visit when I return home?

_____

What personal / self-improvement tasks will I complete?

_____

_____

"Perhaps travel cannot prevent bigotry, but by demonstrating that all peoples cry, laugh, eat, worry, and die, it can introduce the idea that if we try and understand each other, we may even become friends."

– Maya Angelou

What was the best part of today?

_____

_____

What was the best meal I had?

_____

What was better than I expected?

    1.

    2.

    3.

Whom did I meet today?

_____

What did my travel partner enjoy the most? Why?

_____

_____

What do I want to see more of?

_____

_____

Date: **Location:**

What was the best part of today?

_____

_____

What was the best meal I had?

_____

What was better than I expected?

    1.

    2.

    3.

Whom did I meet today?

_____

What did my travel partner enjoy the most? Why?

_____

_____

What do I want to see more of?

_____

_____

What was the best part of today?

_____

_____

What was the best meal I had?

_____

What was better than I expected?

1.

2.

3.

Whom did I meet today?

_____

What did my travel partner enjoy the most? Why?

_____

_____

What do I want to see more of?

_____

_____

Additional Thoughts

_____

_____

_____

_____

What am I missing most from home?

1.

2.

3.

What am I going to eat first when I return home?

_____

What new things will I try when I return home?

_____

Whom will I visit when I return home?

_____

What personal / self-improvement tasks will I complete?

_____

_____

"Why do you go away? So that you can come back.
So that you can see the place you came from with
new eyes and extra colors. And the people there see
you differently, too. Coming back to where you
started is not the same as never leaving."

– **Terry Pratchett**

Date: Location:

What was the best part of today?

_____

_____

What was the best meal I had?

_____

What was better than I expected?

1.

2.

3.

Whom did I meet today?

_____

What did my travel partner enjoy the most? Why?

_____

_____

What do I want to see more of?

_____

_____

What was the best part of today?

_____

_____

What was the best meal I had?

_____

What was better than I expected?

    1.

    2.

    3.

Whom did I meet today?

_____

What did my travel partner enjoy the most? Why?

_____

_____

What do I want to see more of?

_____

_____

What was the best part of today?

_____

_____

What was the best meal I had?

_____

What was better than I expected?

   1.

   2.

   3.

Whom did I meet today?

_____

What did my travel partner enjoy the most? Why?

_____

_____

What do I want to see more of?

_____

_____

Additional Thoughts

_____

_____

_____

_____

What am I missing most from home?

1.

2.

3.

What am I going to eat first when I return home?

_____

What new things will I try when I return home?

_____

Whom will I visit when I return home?

_____

What personal / self-improvement tasks will I complete?

_____

_____

"We travel initially to lose ourselves; and we travel next to find ourselves. We travel to open our hearts and eyes and learn more about the world than our newspapers will accommodate. We travel to bring what little we can, in our ignorance and knowledge, to those parts of the globe where riches are differently dispersed. And we travel, in essence, to become young fools again--to slow time down and get taken in, and to fall in love once more."

– Pico Iyer

What was the best part of today?

_____

_____

What was the best meal I had?

_____

What was better than I expected?

1.

2.

3.

Whom did I meet today?

_____

What did my travel partner enjoy the most? Why?

_____

_____

What do I want to see more of?

_____

_____

What was the best part of today?

_____

_____

What was the best meal I had?

_____

What was better than I expected?

   1.

   2.

   3.

Whom did I meet today?

_____

What did my travel partner enjoy the most? Why?

_____

_____

What do I want to see more of?

_____

_____

What was the best part of today?

_____

_____

What was the best meal I had?

_____

What was better than I expected?

1.

2.

3.

Whom did I meet today?

_____

What did my travel partner enjoy the most? Why?

_____

_____

What do I want to see more of?

_____

_____

> *"The biggest adventure you can take is to live the life of your dreams."* — **Oprah Winfrey**

Additional Thoughts

_____

_____

_____

_____

What am I missing most from home?

1.

2.

3.

What am I going to eat first when I return home?

_____

What new things will I try when I return home?

_____

Whom will I visit when I return home?

_____

What personal / self-improvement tasks will I complete?

_____

_____

"Adventure is a path. Real adventure –
self-determined, self-motivated, often risky – forces
you to have firsthand encounters with the world. The
world the way it is, not the way you imagine it. Your
body will collide with the earth and you will bear
witness. In this way you will be compelled to grapple
with the limitless kindness and bottomless cruelty
of humankind – and perhaps realize that you
yourself are capable of both. This will change you.
Nothing will ever again be black-and-white."

– Mark Jenkins

What was the best part of today?

_____

_____

What was the best meal I had?

_____

What was better than I expected?

1.

2.

3.

Whom did I meet today?

_____

What did my travel partner enjoy the most? Why?

_____

_____

What do I want to see more of?

_____

_____

What was the best part of today?

_____

_____

What was the best meal I had?

_____

What was better than I expected?

1.

2.

3.

Whom did I meet today?

_____

What did my travel partner enjoy the most? Why?

_____

_____

What do I want to see more of?

_____

_____

What was the best part of today?

_____

_____

What was the best meal I had?

_____

What was better than I expected?

    1.

    2.

    3.

Whom did I meet today?

_____

What did my travel partner enjoy the most? Why?

_____

_____

What do I want to see more of?

_____

_____

Additional Thoughts

_____

_____

_____

_____

What am I missing most from home?

1.

2.

3.

What am I going to eat first when I return home?

_____

What new things will I try when I return home?

_____

Whom will I visit when I return home?

_____

What personal / self-improvement tasks will I complete?

_____

_____

"It is a pity that every citizen of each state cannot visit all the others, to see the differences, to learn what we have in common, and come back with a richer, fuller understanding."

– Dwight D. Eisenhower

What was the best part of today?

_____

_____

What was the best meal I had?

_____

What was better than I expected?

1.

2.

3.

Whom did I meet today?

_____

What did my travel partner enjoy the most? Why?

_____

_____

What do I want to see more of?

_____

_____

What was the best part of today?

_____

_____

What was the best meal I had?

_____

What was better than I expected?

    1.

    2.

    3.

Whom did I meet today?

_____

What did my travel partner enjoy the most? Why?

_____

_____

What do I want to see more of?

_____

_____

> *"A ship in harbor is safe, but that is not what ships are built for."* — **John A. Shedd**

What was the best part of today?

_____

_____

What was the best meal I had?

_____

What was better than I expected?

   1.

   2.

   3.

Whom did I meet today?

_____

What did my travel partner enjoy the most? Why?

_____

_____

What do I want to see more of?

_____

_____

Additional Thoughts

_____

_____

_____

_____

What am I missing most from home?

1.

2.

3.

What am I going to eat first when I return home?

_____

What new things will I try when I return home?

_____

Whom will I visit when I return home?

_____

What personal / self-improvement tasks will I complete?

_____

_____

"When we get out of the glass bottle of our ego and when we escape like the squirrels in the cage of our personality and get into the forest again, we shall shiver with cold and fright. But things will happen to us so that we don't know ourselves. Cool, unlying life will rush in."

– D. H. Lawrence

What was the best part of today?

_____

_____

What was the best meal I had?

_____

What was better than I expected?

   1.

   2.

   3.

Whom did I meet today?

_____

What did my travel partner enjoy the most? Why?

_____

_____

What do I want to see more of?

_____

_____

What was the best part of today?

_____

_____

What was the best meal I had?

_____

What was better than I expected?

    1.

    2.

    3.

Whom did I meet today?

_____

What did my travel partner enjoy the most? Why?

_____

_____

What do I want to see more of?

_____

_____

What was the best part of today?

_____

_____

What was the best meal I had?

_____

What was better than I expected?

    1.

    2.

    3.

Whom did I meet today?

_____

What did my travel partner enjoy the most? Why?

_____

_____

What do I want to see more of?

_____

_____

Additional Thoughts

_____

_____

_____

_____

What am I missing most from home?

1.

2.

3.

What am I going to eat first when I return home?

_____

What new things will I try when I return home?

_____

Whom will I visit when I return home?

_____

What personal / self-improvement tasks will I complete?

_____

_____

"I have worn the dust of many foreign streets, but to brush it off would surely be a crime. I have the memories of many foreign adventures, but to forget them, would surely be a sin. So, breathe in the dust, and keep the memories in."

– Rowland Waring-Flood

What was the best part of today?

_____

_____

What was the best meal I had?

_____

What was better than I expected?

1.

2.

3.

Whom did I meet today?

_____

What did my travel partner enjoy the most? Why?

_____

_____

What do I want to see more of?

_____

_____

What was the best part of today?

_____

_____

What was the best meal I had?

_____

What was better than I expected?

1.

2.

3.

Whom did I meet today?

_____

What did my travel partner enjoy the most? Why?

_____

_____

What do I want to see more of?

_____

_____

What was the best part of today?

_____

_____

What was the best meal I had?

_____

What was better than I expected?

    1.

    2.

    3.

Whom did I meet today?

_____

What did my travel partner enjoy the most? Why?

_____

_____

What do I want to see more of?

_____

_____

Additional Thoughts

_____

_____

_____

_____

What am I missing most from home?

1.

2.

3.

What am I going to eat first when I return home?

_____

What new things will I try when I return home?

_____

Whom will I visit when I return home?

_____

What personal / self-improvement tasks will I complete?

_____

_____

"Life should not be a journey to the grave with the intention of arriving safely in a pretty and well-preserved body, but rather to skid in broadside in a cloud of smoke, thoroughly used up, totally worn out, and loudly proclaiming, 'Wow! What a Ride!'"

– Hunter S. Thompson

Date: **Location:**

What was the best part of today?

_____

_____

What was the best meal I had?

_____

What was better than I expected?

    1.

    2.

    3.

Whom did I meet today?

_____

What did my travel partner enjoy the most? Why?

_____

_____

What do I want to see more of?

_____

_____

What was the best part of today?

_____

_____

What was the best meal I had?

_____

What was better than I expected?

1.

2.

3.

Whom did I meet today?

_____

What did my travel partner enjoy the most? Why?

_____

_____

What do I want to see more of?

_____

_____

What was the best part of today?

_____

_____

What was the best meal I had?

_____

What was better than I expected?

    1.

    2.

    3.

Whom did I meet today?

_____

What did my travel partner enjoy the most? Why?

_____

_____

What do I want to see more of?

_____

_____

Additional Thoughts

_____

_____

_____

_____

What am I missing most from home?

1.

2.

3.

What am I going to eat first when I return home?

_____

What new things will I try when I return home?

_____

Whom will I visit when I return home?

_____

What personal / self-improvement tasks will I complete?

_____

_____

"Travel does what good novelists also do to the life of everyday, placing it like a picture in a frame or a gem in its setting, so that the intrinsic qualities are made more clear. Travel does this with the very stuff that everyday life is made of, giving to it the sharp contour and meaning of art."

– Freya Stark

Date: Location:

What was the best part of today?

_____

_____

What was the best meal I had?

_____

What was better than I expected?

1.

2.

3.

Whom did I meet today?

_____

What did my travel partner enjoy the most? Why?

_____

_____

What do I want to see more of?

_____

_____

What was the best part of today?

_____

_____

What was the best meal I had?

_____

What was better than I expected?

1.

2.

3.

Whom did I meet today?

_____

What did my travel partner enjoy the most? Why?

_____

_____

What do I want to see more of?

_____

_____

"May your adventures bring you together, even as they take you far away from home."
Trenton Lee Stewart

What was the best part of today?

_____

_____

What was the best meal I had?

_____

What was better than I expected?

    1.

    2.

    3.

Whom did I meet today?

_____

What did my travel partner enjoy the most? Why?

_____

_____

What do I want to see more of?

_____

_____

Additional Thoughts

_____

_____

_____

_____

What am I missing most from home?

1.

2.

3.

What am I going to eat first when I return home?

_____

What new things will I try when I return home?

_____

Whom will I visit when I return home?

_____

What personal / self-improvement tasks will I complete?

_____

_____

"The whole object of travel is not to set foot on foreign land; it is at last to set foot on one's own country as a foreign land."

– G. K. Chesterton

What was the best part of today?

_____

_____

What was the best meal I had?

_____

What was better than I expected?

   1.

   2.

   3.

Whom did I meet today?

_____

What did my travel partner enjoy the most? Why?

_____

_____

What do I want to see more of?

_____

_____

What was the best part of today?

_____

_____

What was the best meal I had?

_____

What was better than I expected?

1.

2.

3.

Whom did I meet today?

_____

What did my travel partner enjoy the most? Why?

_____

_____

What do I want to see more of?

_____

_____

What was the best part of today?

_____

_____

What was the best meal I had?

_____

What was better than I expected?

1.

2.

3.

Whom did I meet today?

_____

What did my travel partner enjoy the most? Why?

_____

_____

What do I want to see more of?

_____

_____

Additional Thoughts

_____

_____

_____

_____

What am I missing most from home?

1.

2.

3.

What am I going to eat first when I return home?

_____

What new things will I try when I return home?

_____

Whom will I visit when I return home?

_____

What personal / self-improvement tasks will I complete?

_____

_____

"Our happiest moments as tourists always seem to come when we stumble upon one thing while in pursuit of something else."

– Lawrence Block

What was the best part of today?

_____

_____

What was the best meal I had?

_____

What was better than I expected?

    1.

    2.

    3.

Whom did I meet today?

_____

What did my travel partner enjoy the most? Why?

_____

_____

What do I want to see more of?

_____

_____

What was the best part of today?

_____

_____

What was the best meal I had?

_____

What was better than I expected?

    1.

    2.

    3.

Whom did I meet today?

_____

What did my travel partner enjoy the most? Why?

_____

_____

What do I want to see more of?

_____

_____

What was the best part of today?

_____

_____

What was the best meal I had?

_____

What was better than I expected?

    1.

    2.

    3.

Whom did I meet today?

_____

What did my travel partner enjoy the most? Why?

_____

_____

What do I want to see more of?

_____

_____

What was the best part of today?

_____

_____

What was the best meal I had?

_____

What was better than I expected?

    1.

    2.

    3.

Whom did I meet today?

_____

What did my travel partner enjoy the most? Why?

_____

_____

What do I want to see more of?

_____

_____

Additional Thoughts

_____

_____

_____

_____

What am I missing most from home?

   1.

   2.

   3.

What am I going to eat first when I return home?

_____

What new things will I try when I return home?

_____

Whom will I visit when I return home?

_____

What personal / self-improvement tasks will I complete?

_____

_____

"All the pathos and irony of leaving one's youth behind is thus implicit in every joyous moment of travel: one knows that the first joy can never be recovered, and the wise traveler learns not to repeat successes but tries new places all the time."

– Paul Fussell

What was the best part of today?

_____

_____

What was the best meal I had?

_____

What was better than I expected?

    1.

    2.

    3.

Whom did I meet today?

_____

What did my travel partner enjoy the most? Why?

_____

_____

What do I want to see more of?

_____

_____

What was the best part of today?

_____

_____

What was the best meal I had?

_____

What was better than I expected?

    1.

    2.

    3.

Whom did I meet today?

_____

What did my travel partner enjoy the most? Why?

_____

_____

What do I want to see more of?

_____

_____

What was the best part of today?

_____

_____

What was the best meal I had?

_____

What was better than I expected?

1.

2.

3.

Whom did I meet today?

_____

What did my travel partner enjoy the most? Why?

_____

_____

What do I want to see more of?

_____

_____

Additional Thoughts

_____

_____

_____

_____

What am I missing most from home?

1.

2.

3.

What am I going to eat first when I return home?

_____

What new things will I try when I return home?

_____

Whom will I visit when I return home?

_____

What personal / self-improvement tasks will I complete?

_____

_____

"To my mind, the greatest reward and luxury of travel is to be able to experience everyday things as if for the first time, to be in a position in which almost nothing is so familiar it is taken for granted."

– Bill Bryson

Date: Location:

What was the best part of today?

_____

_____

What was the best meal I had?

_____

What was better than I expected?

   1.

   2.

   3.

Whom did I meet today?

_____

What did my travel partner enjoy the most? Why?

_____

_____

What do I want to see more of?

_____

_____

What was the best part of today?

_____

_____

What was the best meal I had?

_____

What was better than I expected?

    1.

    2.

    3.

Whom did I meet today?

_____

What did my travel partner enjoy the most? Why?

_____

_____

What do I want to see more of?

_____

_____

What was the best part of today?

_____

_____

What was the best meal I had?

_____

What was better than I expected?

   1.

   2.

   3.

Whom did I meet today?

_____

What did my travel partner enjoy the most? Why?

_____

_____

What do I want to see more of?

_____

_____

Additional Thoughts

_____

_____

_____

_____

What am I missing most from home?

1.

2.

3.

What am I going to eat first when I return home?

_____

What new things will I try when I return home?

_____

Whom will I visit when I return home?

_____

What personal / self-improvement tasks will I complete?

_____

_____

"We live in a world that is full of beauty, charm and adventure. There is no end to the adventures we can have if only we seek them with our eyes open."

— **Jawaharlal Nehru**

What was the best part of today?

_____

_____

What was the best meal I had?

_____

What was better than I expected?

   1.

   2.

   3.

Whom did I meet today?

_____

What did my travel partner enjoy the most? Why?

_____

_____

What do I want to see more of?

_____

_____

What was the best part of today?

_____

_____

What was the best meal I had?

_____

What was better than I expected?

    1.

    2.

    3.

Whom did I meet today?

_____

What did my travel partner enjoy the most? Why?

_____

_____

What do I want to see more of?

_____

_____

What was the best part of today?

_____

_____

What was the best meal I had?

_____

What was better than I expected?

　1.

　2.

　3.

Whom did I meet today?

_____

What did my travel partner enjoy the most? Why?

_____

_____

What do I want to see more of?

_____

_____

Additional Thoughts

_____

_____

_____

_____

What am I missing most from home?

    1.

    2.

    3.

What am I going to eat first when I return home?

_____

What new things will I try when I return home?

_____

Whom will I visit when I return home?

_____

What personal / self-improvement tasks will I complete?

_____

_____

"To those who stay put, the world is but an imaginary place. But to the movers, the makers, and the shakers, the world is all around, an endless invitation."

– Anonymous

Date: Location:

What was the best part of today?

_____

_____

What was the best meal I had?

_____

What was better than I expected?

   1.

   2.

   3.

Whom did I meet today?

_____

What did my travel partner enjoy the most? Why?

_____

_____

What do I want to see more of?

_____

_____

What was the best part of today?

_____

_____

What was the best meal I had?

_____

What was better than I expected?

    1.

    2.

    3.

Whom did I meet today?

_____

What did my travel partner enjoy the most? Why?

_____

_____

What do I want to see more of?

_____

_____

What was the best part of today?

_____

_____

What was the best meal I had?

_____

What was better than I expected?

1.

2.

3.

Whom did I meet today?

_____

What did my travel partner enjoy the most? Why?

_____

_____

What do I want to see more of?

_____

_____

> *"Don't go where the path may lead; go instead where there is no path and leave a trail."* – **Ralph Waldo Emerson**

Additional Thoughts

_____

_____

_____

_____

What am I missing most from home?

1.

2.

3.

What am I going to eat first when I return home?

_____

What new things will I try when I return home?

_____

Whom will I visit when I return home?

_____

What personal / self-improvement tasks will I complete?

_____

_____

"It is a big and beautiful world. Most of us live and die in the same corner where we were born and never get to see any of it. I don't want to be most of us."

– Oberyn Martell

What was the best part of today?

_____

_____

What was the best meal I had?

_____

What was better than I expected?

1.

2.

3.

Whom did I meet today?

_____

What did my travel partner enjoy the most? Why?

_____

_____

What do I want to see more of?

_____

_____

What was the best part of today?

_____

_____

What was the best meal I had?

_____

What was better than I expected?

1.

2.

3.

Whom did I meet today?

_____

What did my travel partner enjoy the most? Why?

_____

_____

What do I want to see more of?

_____

_____

What was the best part of today?

_____

_____

What was the best meal I had?

_____

What was better than I expected?

1.

2.

3.

Whom did I meet today?

_____

What did my travel partner enjoy the most? Why?

_____

_____

What do I want to see more of?

_____

_____

"We shall not cease from exploration, and at the end of all our exploring will be to arrive where we started and know the place for the first time."

– T.S. Eliot

What was the best part of today?

_____

_____

What was the best meal I had?

_____

What was better than I expected?

1.

2.

3.

Whom did I meet today?

_____

What did my travel partner enjoy the most? Why?

_____

_____

What do I want to see more of?

_____

_____

What was the best part of today?

_____

_____

What was the best meal I had?

_____

What was better than I expected?

   1.

   2.

   3.

Whom did I meet today?

_____

What did my travel partner enjoy the most? Why?

_____

_____

What do I want to see more of?

_____

_____

What was the best part of today?

_____

_____

What was the best meal I had?

_____

What was better than I expected?

   1.

   2.

   3.

Whom did I meet today?

_____

What did my travel partner enjoy the most? Why?

_____

_____

What do I want to see more of?

_____

_____

Additional Thoughts

_____

_____

_____

_____

What am I missing most from home?

1.

2.

3.

What am I going to eat first when I return home?

_____

What new things will I try when I return home?

_____

Whom will I visit when I return home?

_____

What personal / self-improvement tasks will I complete?

_____

_____

"I travel because it makes me realize how much I haven't seen, how much I'm not going to see, and how much I still need to see."

– Carew Papritz

What was the best part of today?

_____

_____

What was the best meal I had?

_____

What was better than I expected?

    1.

    2.

    3.

Whom did I meet today?

_____

What did my travel partner enjoy the most? Why?

_____

_____

What do I want to see more of?

_____

_____

What was the best part of today?

_____

_____

What was the best meal I had?

_____

What was better than I expected?

    1.

    2.

    3.

Whom did I meet today?

_____

What did my travel partner enjoy the most? Why?

_____

_____

What do I want to see more of?

_____

_____

What was the best part of today?

_____

_____

What was the best meal I had?

_____

What was better than I expected?

   1.

   2.

   3.

Whom did I meet today?

_____

What did my travel partner enjoy the most? Why?

_____

_____

What do I want to see more of?

_____

_____

Additional Thoughts

_____

_____

_____

_____

What am I missing most from home?

1.

2.

3.

What am I going to eat first when I return home?

_____

What new things will I try when I return home?

_____

Whom will I visit when I return home?

_____

What personal / self-improvement tasks will I complete?

_____

_____

"There is freedom waiting for you, on the breezes of the sky. And you ask, 'what if I fall?' Oh, but my darling, what if you fly?"

– Erin Hanson

What was the best part of today?

_____

_____

What was the best meal I had?

_____

What was better than I expected?

   1.

   2.

   3.

Whom did I meet today?

_____

What did my travel partner enjoy the most? Why?

_____

_____

What do I want to see more of?

_____

_____

What was the best part of today?

_____

_____

What was the best meal I had?

_____

What was better than I expected?

1.

2.

3.

Whom did I meet today?

_____

What did my travel partner enjoy the most? Why?

_____

_____

What do I want to see more of?

_____

_____

What was the best part of today?

_____

_____

What was the best meal I had?

_____

What was better than I expected?

1.

2.

3.

Whom did I meet today?

_____

What did my travel partner enjoy the most? Why?

_____

_____

What do I want to see more of?

_____

_____

Additional Thoughts

_____

_____

_____

_____

What am I missing most from home?

1.

2.

3.

What am I going to eat first when I return home?

_____

What new things will I try when I return home?

_____

Whom will I visit when I return home?

_____

What personal / self-improvement tasks will I complete?

_____

_____

"Life is not measured by the number of breaths we take, but by the moments and places that take our breath away."

– Anonymous

What was the best part of today?

_____

_____

What was the best meal I had?

_____

What was better than I expected?

    1.

    2.

    3.

Whom did I meet today?

_____

What did my travel partner enjoy the most? Why?

_____

_____

What do I want to see more of?

_____

_____

What was the best part of today?

_____

_____

What was the best meal I had?

_____

What was better than I expected?

1.

2.

3.

Whom did I meet today?

_____

What did my travel partner enjoy the most? Why?

_____

_____

What do I want to see more of?

_____

_____

What was the best part of today?

_____

_____

What was the best meal I had?

_____

What was better than I expected?

1.

2.

3.

Whom did I meet today?

_____

What did my travel partner enjoy the most? Why?

_____

_____

What do I want to see more of?

_____

_____

Additional Thoughts

_____

_____

_____

_____

What am I missing most from home?

1.

2.

3.

What am I going to eat first when I return home?

_____

What new things will I try when I return home?

_____

Whom will I visit when I return home?

_____

What personal / self-improvement tasks will I complete?

_____

_____

"The border means more than a customs house, a passport officer, a man with a gun. Over there everything is going to be different; life is never going to be quite the same again after your passport has been stamped."

— **Graham Greene**

Date: Location:

What was the best part of today?

_____

_____

What was the best meal I had?

_____

What was better than I expected?

1.

2.

3.

Whom did I meet today?

_____

What did my travel partner enjoy the most? Why?

_____

_____

What do I want to see more of?

_____

_____

What was the best part of today?

_____

_____

What was the best meal I had?

_____

What was better than I expected?

    1.

    2.

    3.

Whom did I meet today?

_____

What did my travel partner enjoy the most? Why?

_____

_____

What do I want to see more of?

_____

_____

What was the best part of today?

_____

_____

What was the best meal I had?

_____

What was better than I expected?

    1.

    2.

    3.

Whom did I meet today?

_____

What did my travel partner enjoy the most? Why?

_____

_____

What do I want to see more of?

_____

_____

Additional Thoughts

_____

_____

_____

_____

What am I missing most from home?

    1.

    2.

    3.

What am I going to eat first when I return home?

_____

What new things will I try when I return home?

_____

Whom will I visit when I return home?

_____

What personal / self-improvement tasks will I complete?

_____

_____

"The tragedy in the lives of most of us is that we go through life walking down a high-walled lane with people of our own kind, the same economic situation, the same national background and education and religious outlook. And beyond those walls, all humanity lies, unknown and unseen, and untouched by our restricted and impoverished lives."

— **Florence Luscomb**

What was the best part of today?

_____

_____

What was the best meal I had?

_____

What was better than I expected?

    1.

    2.

    3.

Whom did I meet today?

_____

What did my travel partner enjoy the most? Why?

_____

_____

What do I want to see more of?

_____

_____

Additional Thoughts

_____

_____

_____

_____

What am I missing most from home?

1.

2.

3.

What am I going to eat first when I return home?

_____

What new things will I try when I return home?

_____

Whom will I visit when I return home?

_____

What personal / self-improvement tasks will I complete?

_____

_____

"For me, a place unvisited is like an unrequited love. A dull ache that—try as you might to think it away, to convince yourself that she really wasn't the right country for you—just won't leave you in peace."

— **Eric Weiner**

What was the best part of today?

_____

_____

What was the best meal I had?

_____

What was better than I expected?

1.

2.

3.

Whom did I meet today?

_____

What did my travel partner enjoy the most? Why?

_____

_____

What do I want to see more of?

_____

_____

What was the best part of today?

_____

_____

What was the best meal I had?

_____

What was better than I expected?

   1.

   2.

   3.

Whom did I meet today?

_____

What did my travel partner enjoy the most? Why?

_____

_____

What do I want to see more of?

_____

_____

What was the best part of today?

_____

_____

What was the best meal I had?

_____

What was better than I expected?

1.

2.

3.

Whom did I meet today?

_____

What did my travel partner enjoy the most? Why?

_____

_____

What do I want to see more of?

_____

_____

Additional Thoughts

_____

_____

_____

_____

What am I missing most from home?

1.

2.

3.

What am I going to eat first when I return home?

_____

What new things will I try when I return home?

_____

Whom will I visit when I return home?

_____

What personal / self-improvement tasks will I complete?

_____

_____

"Our footprints always follow us on days when it's been snowing. They always show us where we've been, but never show us where we're going."

– Winnie the Pooh

What was the best part of today?

_____

_____

What was the best meal I had?

_____

What was better than I expected?

1.

2.

3.

Whom did I meet today?

_____

What did my travel partner enjoy the most? Why?

_____

_____

What do I want to see more of?

_____

_____

What was the best part of today?

_____

_____

What was the best meal I had?

_____

What was better than I expected?

    1.

    2.

    3.

Whom did I meet today?

_____

What did my travel partner enjoy the most? Why?

_____

_____

What do I want to see more of?

_____

_____

What was the best part of today?

_____

_____

What was the best meal I had?

_____

What was better than I expected?

    1.

    2.

    3.

Whom did I meet today?

_____

What did my travel partner enjoy the most? Why?

_____

_____

What do I want to see more of?

_____

_____

Additional Thoughts

_____

_____

_____

_____

What am I missing most from home?

1.

2.

3.

What am I going to eat first when I return home?

_____

What new things will I try when I return home?

_____

Whom will I visit when I return home?

_____

What personal / self-improvement tasks will I complete?

_____

_____

"Traveler, there is no path.

The path is made by walking.

By walking you make a path

And turning, you look back

At a way you will never tread again"

— **Antonio Machado**

What was the best part of today?

_____

_____

What was the best meal I had?

_____

What was better than I expected?

   1.

   2.

   3.

Whom did I meet today?

_____

What did my travel partner enjoy the most? Why?

_____

_____

What do I want to see more of?

_____

_____

What was the best part of today?

_____

_____

What was the best meal I had?

_____

What was better than I expected?

    1.

    2.

    3.

Whom did I meet today?

_____

What did my travel partner enjoy the most? Why?

_____

_____

What do I want to see more of?

_____

_____

> *"It's good to have an end to journey toward, but it is the journey that matters in the end."* — **Ernest Hemingway**

What was the best part of today?

_____

_____

What was the best meal I had?

_____

What was better than I expected?

    1.

    2.

    3.

Whom did I meet today?

_____

What did my travel partner enjoy the most? Why?

_____

_____

What do I want to see more of?

_____

_____

Additional Thoughts

_____

_____

_____

_____

What am I missing most from home?

1.

2.

3.

What am I going to eat first when I return home?

_____

What new things will I try when I return home?

_____

Whom will I visit when I return home?

_____

What personal / self-improvement tasks will I complete?

_____

_____

"All men have the stars," he answered, "but they are not the same things for different people. For some, who are travellers, the stars are guides. For others they are no more than little lights in the sky. For others, who are scholars, they are problems. For my businessman they were wealth. But all the stars are silent. You—you alone—will have the stars as no one else has them."

— **The Little Prince**

What was the best part of today?

_____

_____

What was the best meal I had?

_____

What was better than I expected?

    1.

    2.

    3.

Whom did I meet today?

_____

What did my travel partner enjoy the most? Why?

_____

_____

What do I want to see more of?

_____

_____

What was the best part of today?

_____

_____

What was the best meal I had?

_____

What was better than I expected?

    1.

    2.

    3.

Whom did I meet today?

_____

What did my travel partner enjoy the most? Why?

_____

_____

What do I want to see more of?

_____

_____

What was the best part of today?

_____

_____

What was the best meal I had?

_____

What was better than I expected?

   1.

   2.

   3.

Whom did I meet today?

_____

What did my travel partner enjoy the most? Why?

_____

_____

What do I want to see more of?

_____

_____

Additional Thoughts

_____

_____

_____

_____

What am I missing most from home?

    1.

    2.

    3.

What am I going to eat first when I return home?

_____

What new things will I try when I return home?

_____

Whom will I visit when I return home?

_____

What personal / self-improvement tasks will I complete?

_____

_____

"Every time you leave home,
Another road takes you
Into a world you were never in.
New strangers on other paths await.
New places that have never seen you
Will startle a little at your entry
Old places that know you well
Will pretend nothing
Changed since your last visit."

-John O'Donohue

What was the best part of today?

_____

_____

What was the best meal I had?

_____

What was better than I expected?

    1.

    2.

    3.

Whom did I meet today?

_____

What did my travel partner enjoy the most? Why?

_____

_____

What do I want to see more of?

_____

_____

What was the best part of today?

_____

_____

What was the best meal I had?

_____

What was better than I expected?

    1.

    2.

    3.

Whom did I meet today?

_____

What did my travel partner enjoy the most? Why?

_____

_____

What do I want to see more of?

_____

_____

What was the best part of today?

_____

_____

What was the best meal I had?

_____

What was better than I expected?

1.

2.

3.

Whom did I meet today?

_____

What did my travel partner enjoy the most? Why?

_____

_____

What do I want to see more of?

_____

_____

Additional Thoughts

_____

_____

_____

_____

What am I missing most from home?

1.

2.

3.

What am I going to eat first when I return home?

_____

What new things will I try when I return home?

_____

Whom will I visit when I return home?

_____

What personal / self-improvement tasks will I complete?

_____

_____

"Every place is a goldmine. You have only to give yourself time, sit in a teahouse watching the passers-by, stand in a corner of the market, go for a haircut. You pick up a thread—a word, a meeting, a friend of a friend of someone you have just met—and soon the most insipid, most insignificant place becomes a mirror of the world, a window on life, a theatre of humanity."

— **Tiziano Terzani**

Date: **Location:**

What was the best part of today?

_____

_____

What was the best meal I had?

_____

What was better than I expected?

    1.

    2.

    3.

Whom did I meet today?

_____

What did my travel partner enjoy the most? Why?

_____

_____

What do I want to see more of?

_____

_____

What was the best part of today?

_____

_____

What was the best meal I had?

_____

What was better than I expected?

1.

2.

3.

Whom did I meet today?

_____

What did my travel partner enjoy the most? Why?

_____

_____

What do I want to see more of?

_____

_____

Date: Location:

What was the best part of today?

_____

_____

What was the best meal I had?

_____

What was better than I expected?

1.

2.

3.

Whom did I meet today?

_____

What did my travel partner enjoy the most? Why?

_____

_____

What do I want to see more of?

_____

_____

Additional Thoughts

_____

_____

_____

_____

What am I missing most from home?

1.

2.

3.

What am I going to eat first when I return home?

_____

What new things will I try when I return home?

_____

Whom will I visit when I return home?

_____

What personal / self-improvement tasks will I complete?

_____

_____

"Travel is like love, mostly because it's a heightened state of awareness, in which we are mindful, receptive, undimmed by familiarity and ready to be transformed. That is why the best trips, like the best love affairs, never really end."

— **Pico Iyer**

Date: _____ Location: _____

What was the best part of today?

_____

_____

What was the best meal I had?

_____

What was better than I expected?

1.

2.

3.

Whom did I meet today?

_____

What did my travel partner enjoy the most? Why?

_____

_____

What do I want to see more of?

_____

_____

What was the best part of today?

_____

_____

What was the best meal I had?

_____

What was better than I expected?

1.

2.

3.

Whom did I meet today?

_____

What did my travel partner enjoy the most? Why?

_____

_____

What do I want to see more of?

_____

_____

Additional Thoughts

_____

_____

_____

_____

What am I missing most from home?

1.

2.

3.

What am I going to eat first when I return home?

_____

What new things will I try when I return home?

_____

Whom will I visit when I return home?

_____

What personal / self-improvement tasks will I complete?

_____

_____

"We shall not cease from exploration
And at the end of all our exploring
Will be to arrive at the place that we started
And know the place for the first time."

-T.S. Eliot

Date: _____ Location: _____

What was the best part of today?

_____

_____

What was the best meal I had?

_____

What was better than I expected?

1.

2.

3.

Whom did I meet today?

_____

What did my travel partner enjoy the most? Why?

_____

_____

What do I want to see more of?

_____

_____

Date: Location:

What was the best part of today?

_____

_____

What was the best meal I had?

_____

What was better than I expected?

    1.

    2.

    3.

Whom did I meet today?

_____

What did my travel partner enjoy the most? Why?

_____

_____

What do I want to see more of?

_____

_____

What was the best part of today?

_____

_____

What was the best meal I had?

_____

What was better than I expected?

    1.

    2.

    3.

Whom did I meet today?

_____

What did my travel partner enjoy the most? Why?

_____

_____

What do I want to see more of?

_____

_____

Additional Thoughts

_____

_____

_____

_____

What am I missing most from home?

1.

2.

3.

What am I going to eat first when I return home?

_____

What new things will I try when I return home?

_____

Whom will I visit when I return home?

_____

What personal / self-improvement tasks will I complete?

_____

_____

Thank You!

To thank you for taking the time to read my book, I am offering a free video to help you save some serious cash on your next trip!

FREE VIDEO
How to find destinations with the lowest airfares!

Learn how to find the cheapest places in the world to fly. Choose your next travel destination based on the lowest fares--anywhere in the world! To get access to the video, go to https://www.internationaltravelsecrets.com/free-video

Now that you have gained some in-depth knowledge on international travel, I invite you to keep the adventure going. Need some help booking that next trip? I can help!

ONLINE COURSES

Let me show you step-by-step how to book cheap flights around the world, find hotels in the best places, and choose tours that fit your needs. These courses will take you deeper into the information presented in this book and hold your hand in the process, so you don't miss a step. Go to https://www.internationaltravelsecrets.com/online-courses

TRIP PLANNING SERVICES

Stuck while trying to plan your next trip? Book a one-on-one consult to get the answers you need to finish booking your dream trip to spots all over the world. I am happy to assist. Go to https://www.internationaltravelsecrets.com/travel-with-me

TRAVEL WITH ME - ORGANIZED GROUP TRIPS

Don't want to spend the time researching and planning your next trip? Let me do the work for you in organizing the best flights, hotels, landmarks, visa requirements, ground transportation, and everything else you need to complete before visiting that country on your bucket list. Join me and a small group of travelers to visit destinations around the world. All you have to do is show up. Go to https://www.internationaltravelsecrets.com/travel-with-me

DON'T GO YET!

I NEED YOUR HELP!

I really appreciate your feedback and love hearing what you have to say. I need your input to make the next version of this journal and my future books better.

Please leave me a helpful review on Amazon letting me know what you think of the journal.

Please also recommend this journal to anyone you know who can benefit from recording their travel memories. Let's get more people traveling the world!

Thank you so much!

-Michael Wedaa

A PERFECT COMPANION TO THE BEST-SELLING BOOK
International Travel Secrets

International Travel Secrets has step-by-step instructions on finding rock-bottom prices on travel--without booking last-minute or staying in crowded hostels. A must read for beginning travelers and seasoned travelers alike. Find out how to see a country in 2 days and how to use layovers as a tool to see more countries--for free! Learn how to avoid baggage fees, ATM fees, and foreign transaction fees. Master how to determine which countries are safe and how to protect yourself in a robbery. Learn how to negotiate prices, which credit cards to use, how to get free travel insurance, and much more!

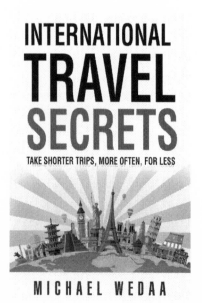

Made in the USA
Coppell, TX
12 February 2022